NEVER FORGET: HEROES OF 9/11

FIGHTING BACK IN FLIGHT

BY JAMES BUCKLEY JR.

ILLUSTRATED BY ANDY DUGGAN

BEARPORT
PUBLISHING

Minneapolis, Minnesota

BEAR CLAW

Credits

21 top, © Diane Bondareff/AP Photo; 21 center © Dan Lopez/The Daily Progress/AP Photo; 21 bottom © Gene Puskar/AP Photo; 22, © Jeffrey Isaac Greenberg/Alamy Stock Photo.

Bearport Publishing Company
Minneapolis, Minnesota
President: Jen Jenson
Director of Product Development: Spencer Brinker
Senior Editor: Allison Juda
Associate Editor: Charly Haley

Produced by Shoreline Publishing Group LLC
Santa Barbara, California
Designer: Patty Kelley
Editorial Director: James Buckley Jr.

DISCLAIMER: On September 11, 2001, the United States was attacked, and 2,977 people died. This graphic story is a dramatization based on true events of that day. It is intended to give the reader a sense of the narrative rather than a presentation of actual details as they occurred. It is also intended to honor those who lost their lives and to celebrate the heroic efforts of so many on a day that the world will never forget.

Library of Congress Cataloging-in-Publication Data is available at www.loc.gov or upon request from the publisher.

ISBN: 978-1-63691-027-7 (hardcover)
ISBN: 978-1-63691-034-5 (paperback)
ISBN: 978-1-63691-041-3 (ebook)

For more information, write to Bearport Publishing, 5357 Penn Avenue South, Minneapolis, MN 55419.
Printed in the United States of America.

Contents

Chapter 1
INTO THE AIR

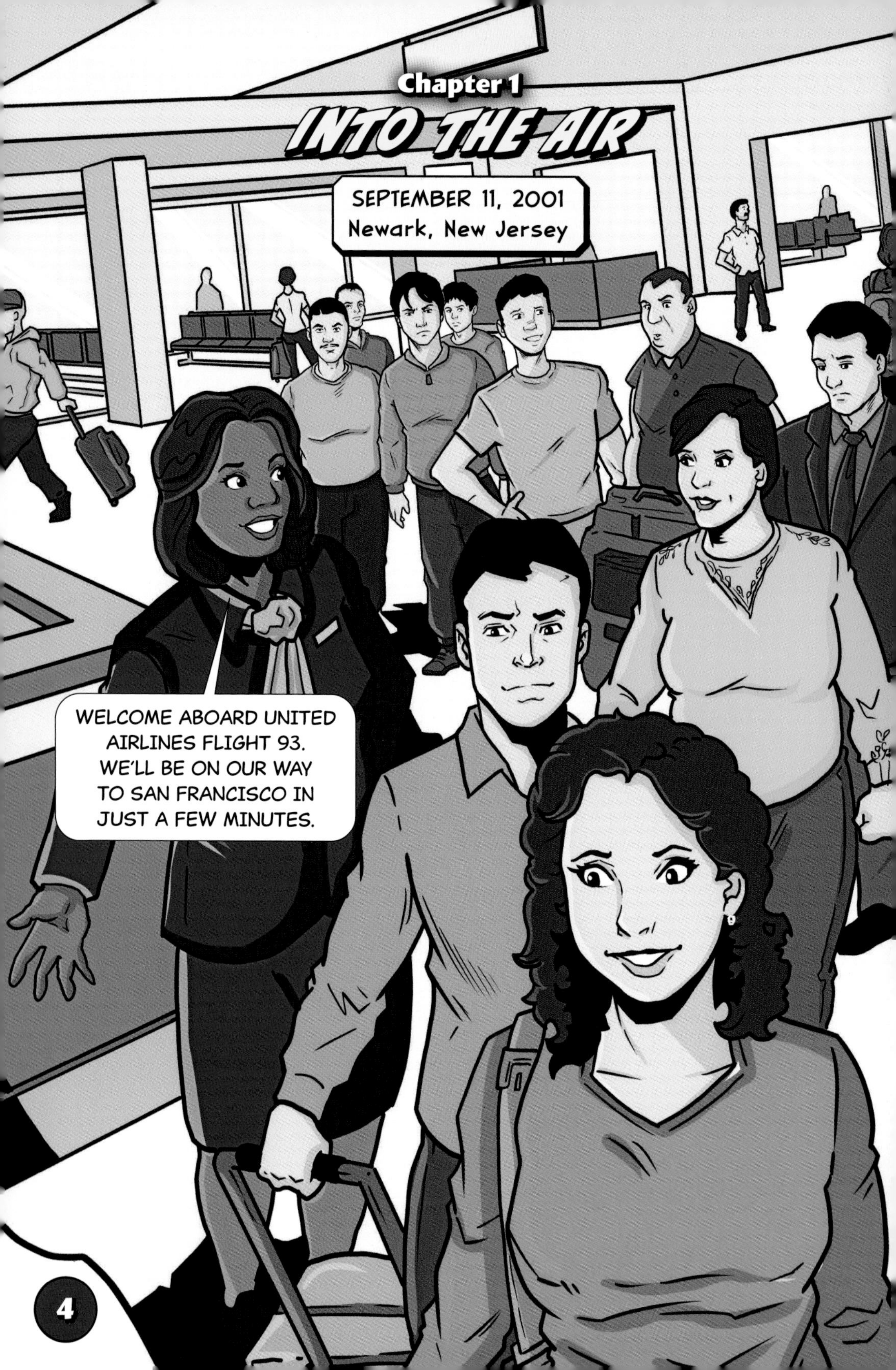
SEPTEMBER 11, 2001
Newark, New Jersey
WELCOME ABOARD UNITED AIRLINES FLIGHT 93. WE'LL BE ON OUR WAY TO SAN FRANCISCO IN JUST A FEW MINUTES.

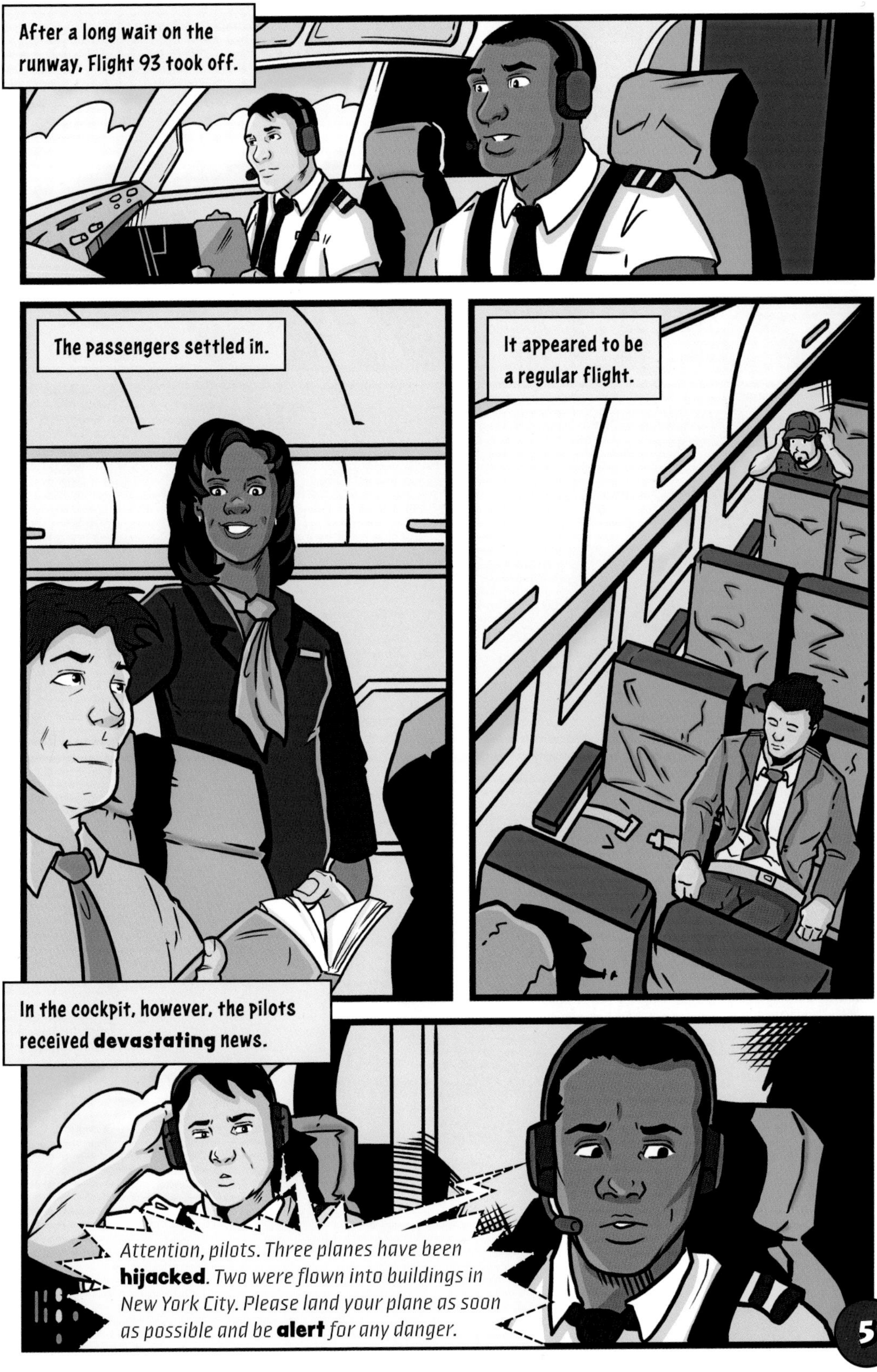
After a long wait on the runway, Flight 93 took off.
The passengers settled in.
It appeared to be a regular flight.
In the cockpit, however, the pilots received **devastating** news.
Attention, pilots. Three planes have been **hijacked**. *Two were flown into buildings in New York City. Please land your plane as soon as possible and be* **alert** *for any danger.*

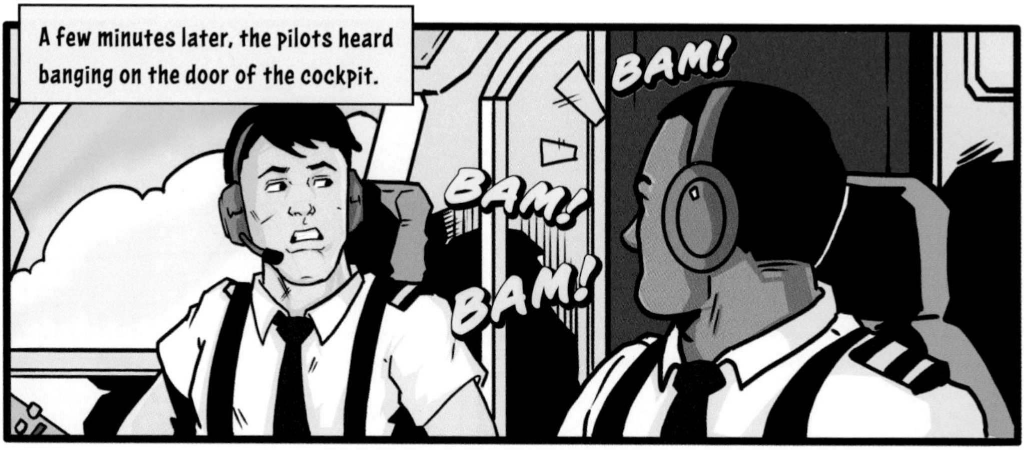
A few minutes later, the pilots heard banging on the door of the cockpit.
BAM!
BAM!
BAM!

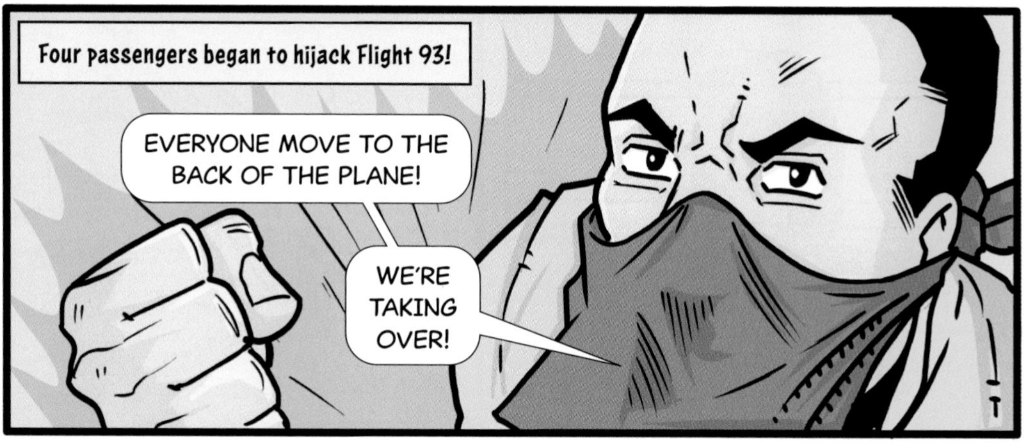
Four passengers began to hijack Flight 93!
EVERYONE MOVE TO THE BACK OF THE PLANE!
WE'RE TAKING OVER!

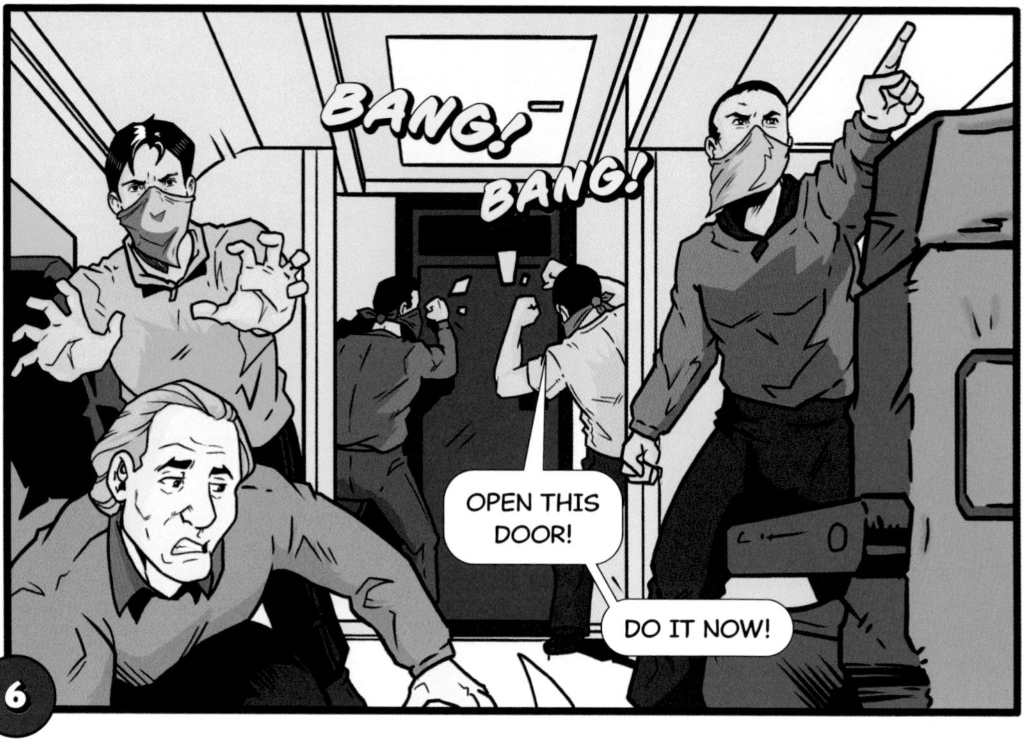
BANG!
BANG!
OPEN THIS DOOR!
DO IT NOW!

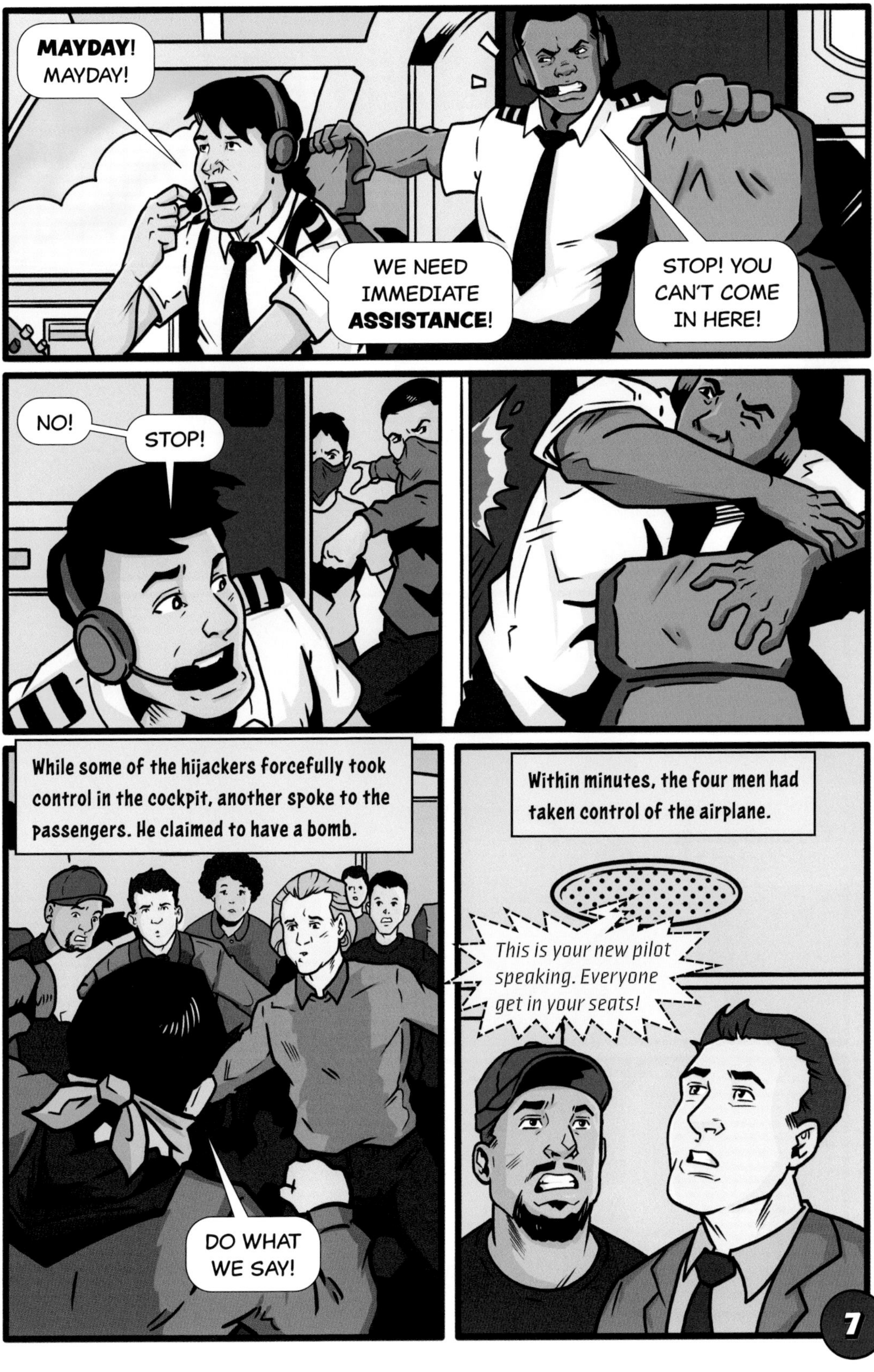

MAYDAY! MAYDAY!
WE NEED IMMEDIATE ASSISTANCE!
STOP! YOU CAN'T COME IN HERE!
NO!
STOP!
While some of the hijackers forcefully took control in the cockpit, another spoke to the passengers. He claimed to have a bomb.
DO WHAT WE SAY!
Within minutes, the four men had taken control of the airplane.
This is your new pilot speaking. Everyone get in your seats!

Chapter 2

A DESPERATE PLAN

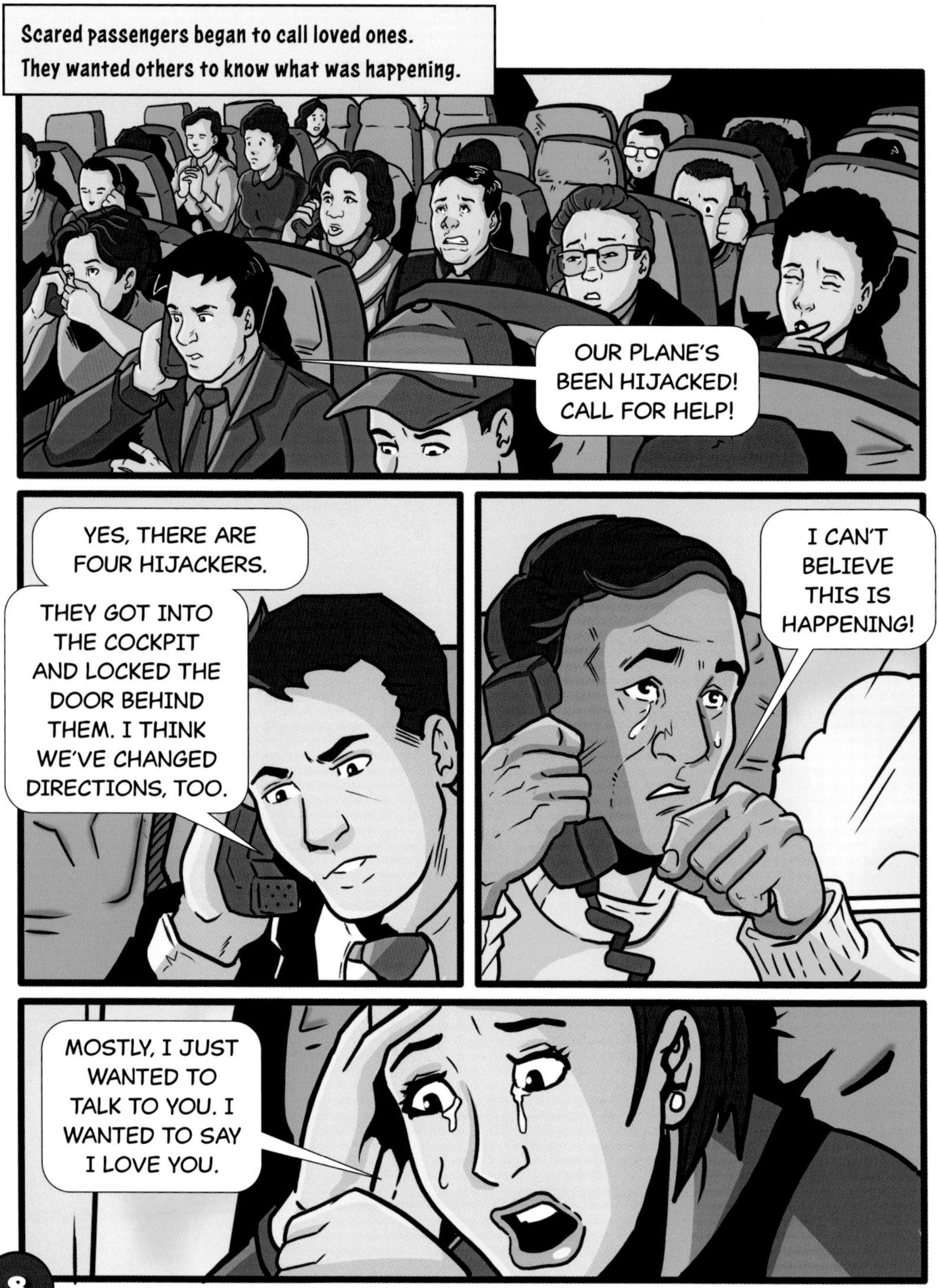
Scared passengers began to call loved ones. They wanted others to know what was happening.
OUR PLANE'S BEEN HIJACKED! CALL FOR HELP!
YES, THERE ARE FOUR HIJACKERS.
THEY GOT INTO THE COCKPIT AND LOCKED THE DOOR BEHIND THEM. I THINK WE'VE CHANGED DIRECTIONS, TOO.
I CAN'T BELIEVE THIS IS HAPPENING!
MOSTLY, I JUST WANTED TO TALK TO YOU. I WANTED TO SAY I LOVE YOU.

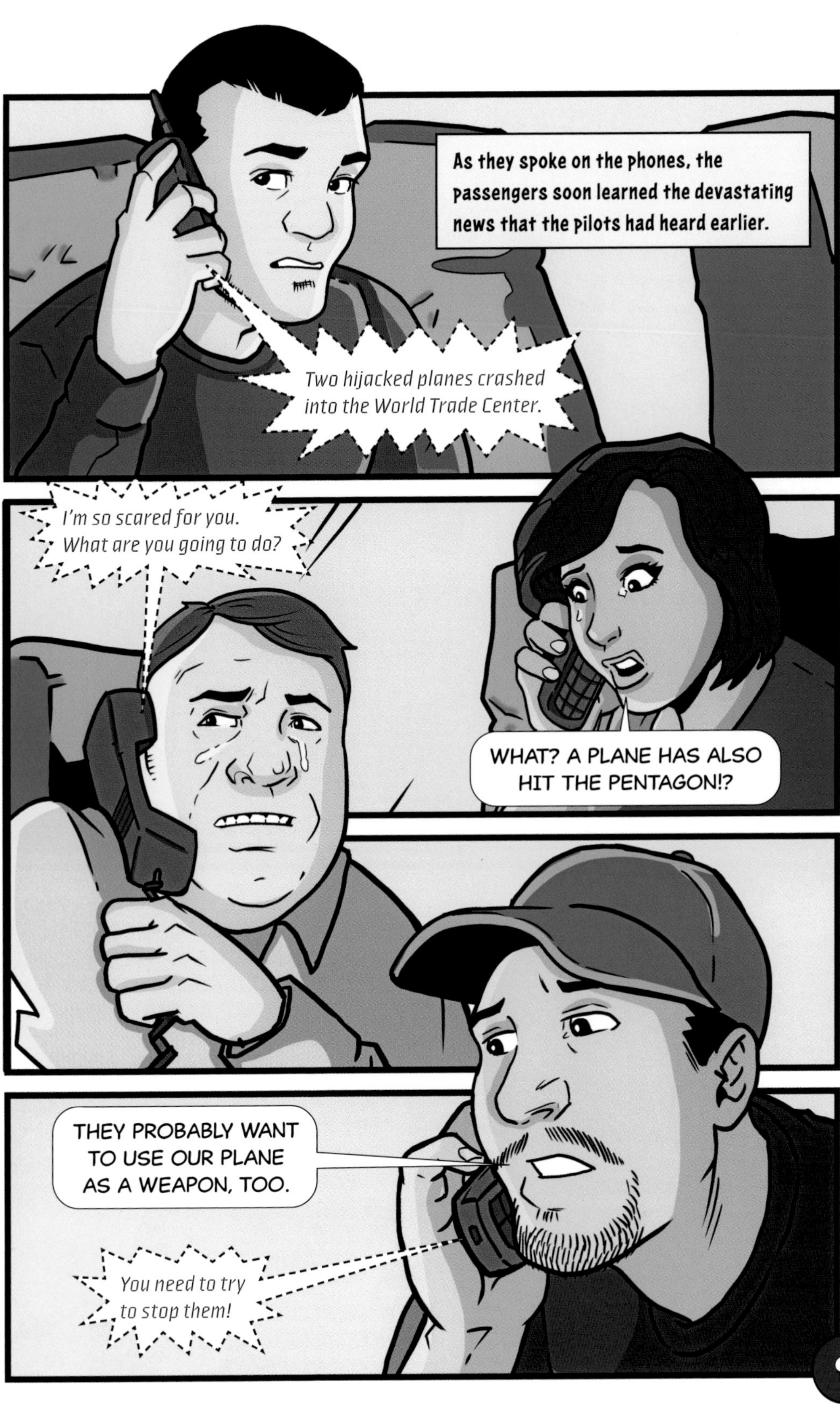
As they spoke on the phones, the passengers soon learned the devastating news that the pilots had heard earlier.
Two hijacked planes crashed into the World Trade Center.
I'm so scared for you. What are you going to do?
WHAT? A PLANE HAS ALSO HIT THE PENTAGON!?
THEY PROBABLY WANT TO USE OUR PLANE AS A WEAPON, TOO.
You need to try to stop them!

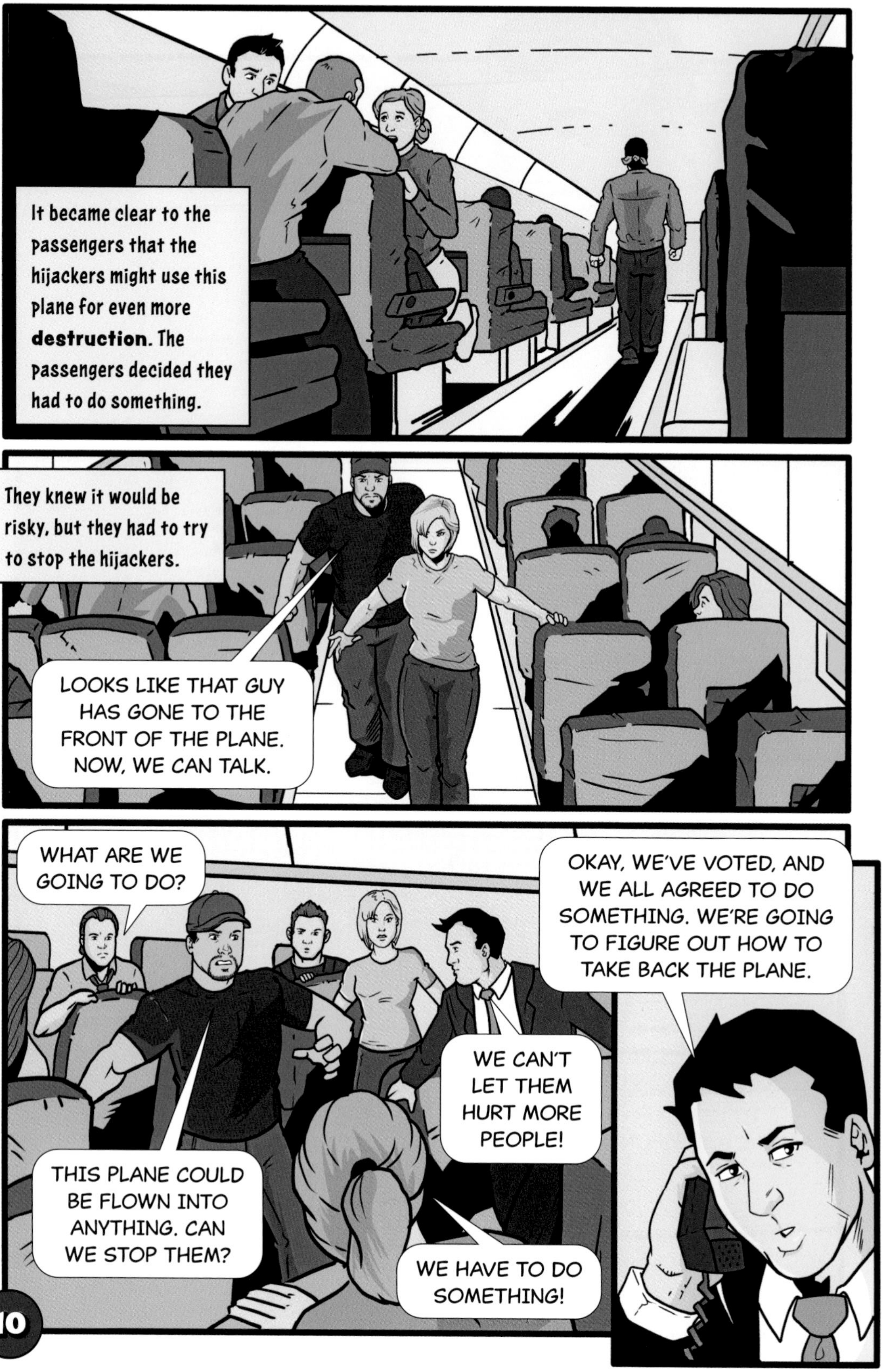
It became clear to the passengers that the hijackers might use this plane for even more **destruction**. The passengers decided they had to do something.
They knew it would be risky, but they had to try to stop the hijackers.
LOOKS LIKE THAT GUY HAS GONE TO THE FRONT OF THE PLANE. NOW, WE CAN TALK.
WHAT ARE WE GOING TO DO?
THIS PLANE COULD BE FLOWN INTO ANYTHING. CAN WE STOP THEM?
WE CAN'T LET THEM HURT MORE PEOPLE!
WE HAVE TO DO SOMETHING!
OKAY, WE'VE VOTED, AND WE ALL AGREED TO DO SOMETHING. WE'RE GOING TO FIGURE OUT HOW TO TAKE BACK THE PLANE.

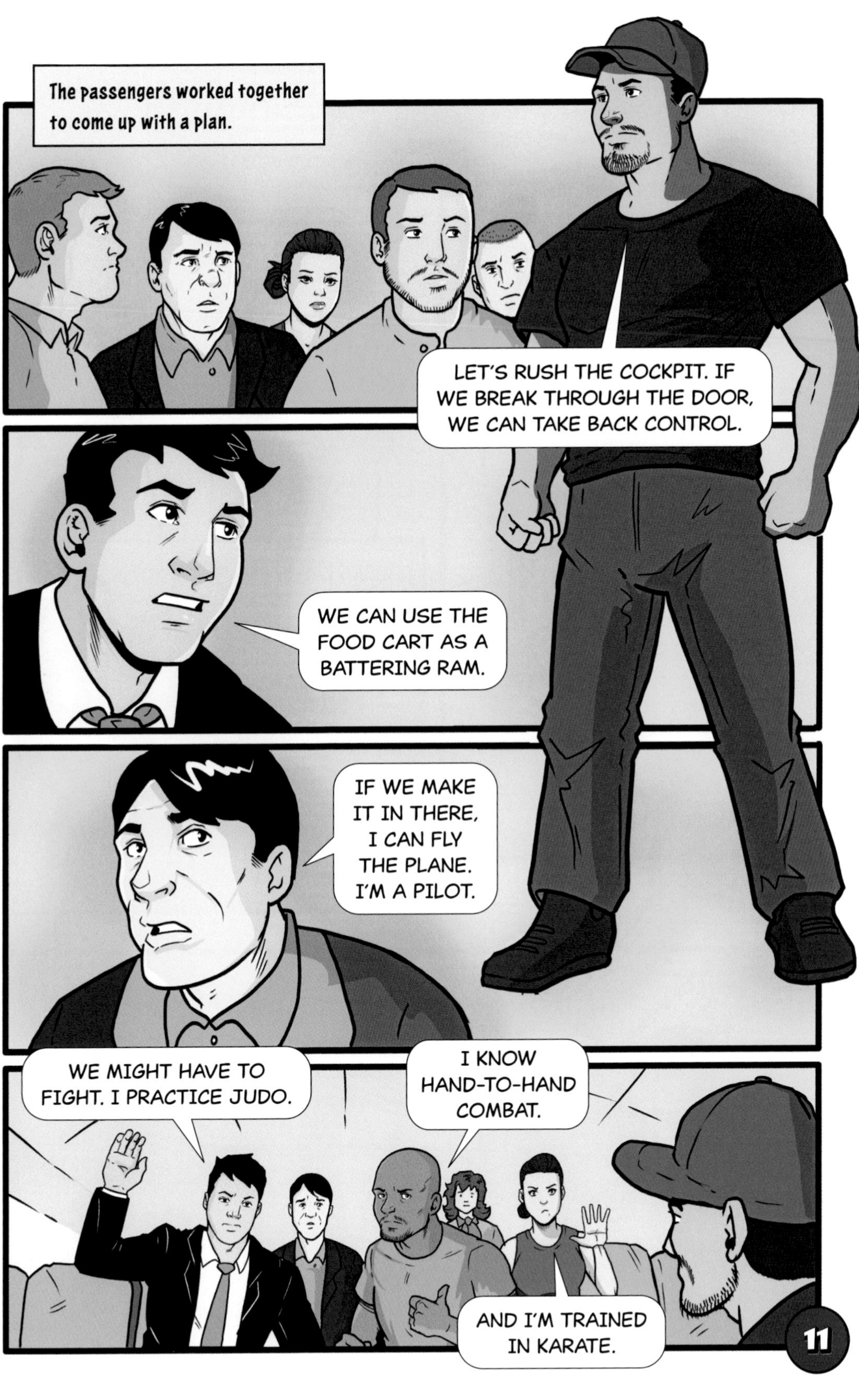
The passengers worked together to come up with a plan.
LET'S RUSH THE COCKPIT. IF WE BREAK THROUGH THE DOOR, WE CAN TAKE BACK CONTROL.
WE CAN USE THE FOOD CART AS A BATTERING RAM.
IF WE MAKE IT IN THERE, I CAN FLY THE PLANE. I'M A PILOT.
WE MIGHT HAVE TO FIGHT. I PRACTICE JUDO.
I KNOW HAND-TO-HAND COMBAT.
AND I'M TRAINED IN KARATE.

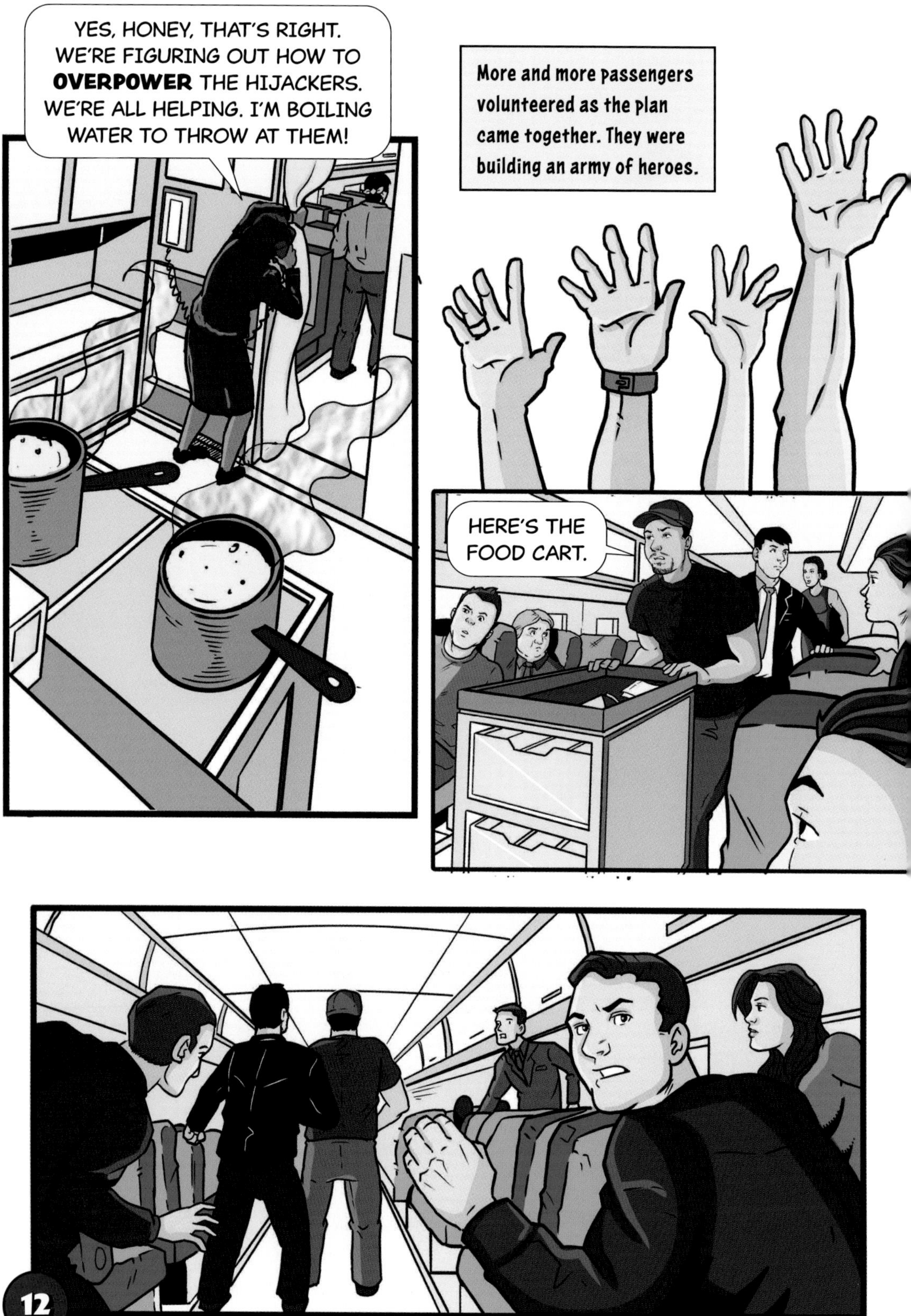
YES, HONEY, THAT'S RIGHT. WE'RE FIGURING OUT HOW TO **OVERPOWER** THE HIJACKERS. WE'RE ALL HELPING. I'M BOILING WATER TO THROW AT THEM!
More and more passengers volunteered as the plan came together. They were building an army of heroes.
HERE'S THE FOOD CART.

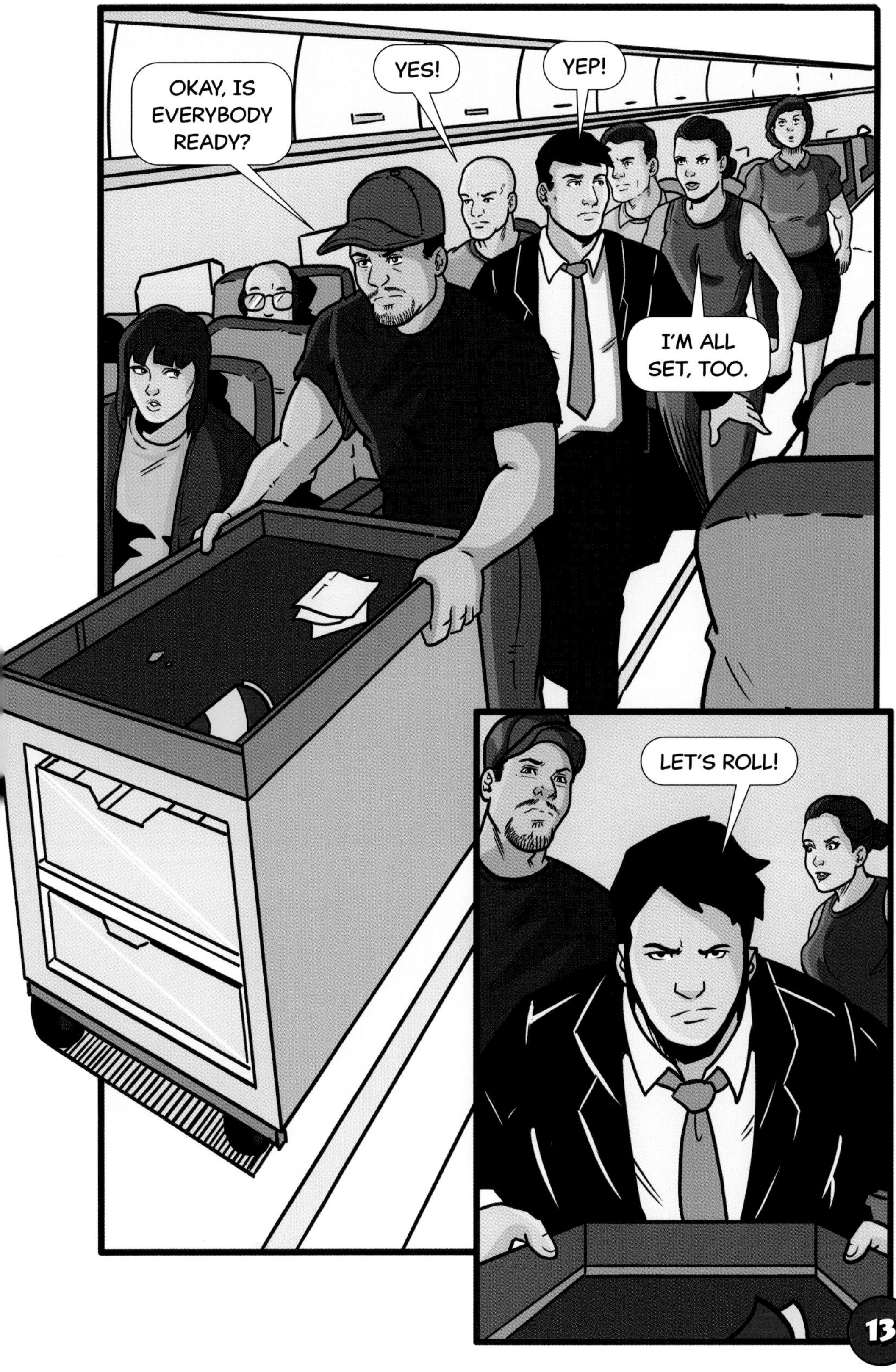
OKAY, IS EVERYBODY READY?
YES!
YEP!
I'M ALL SET, TOO.
LET'S ROLL!

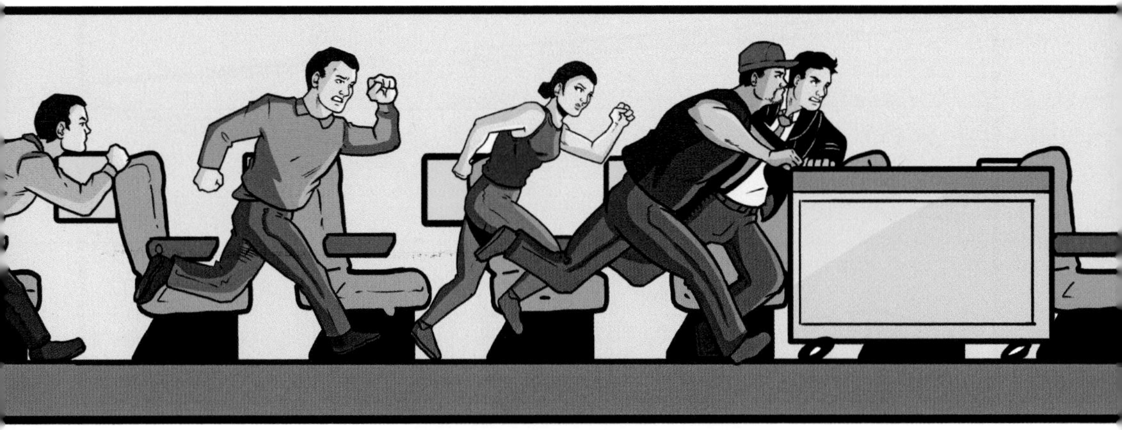

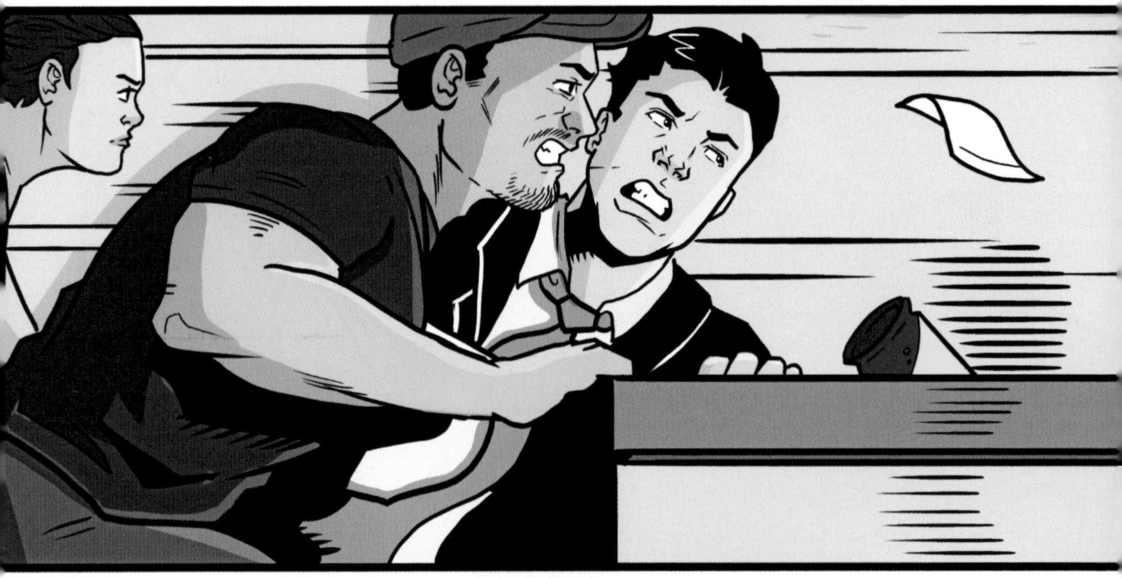

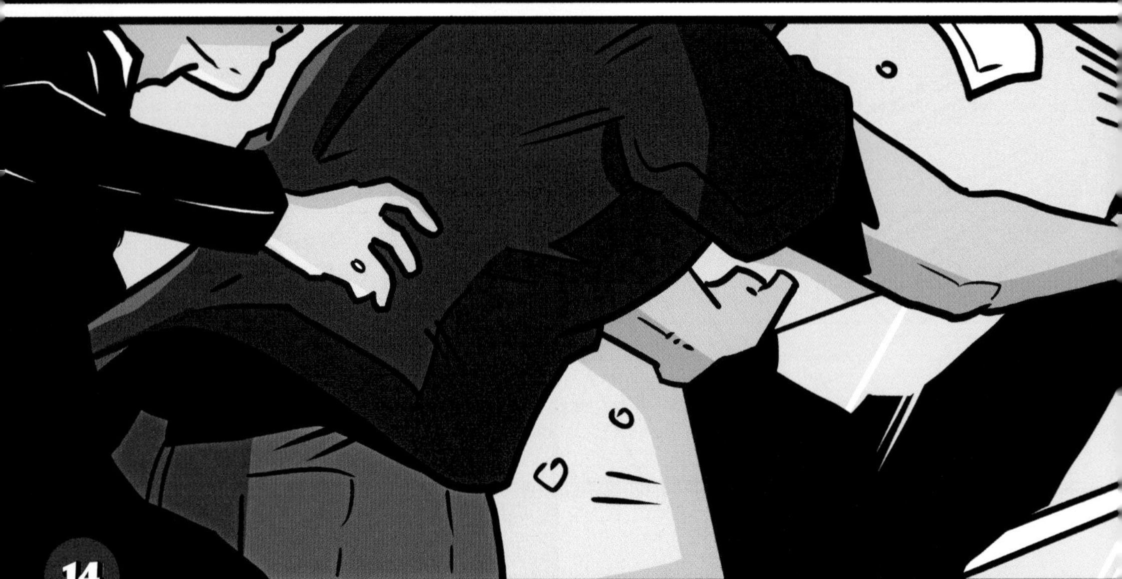

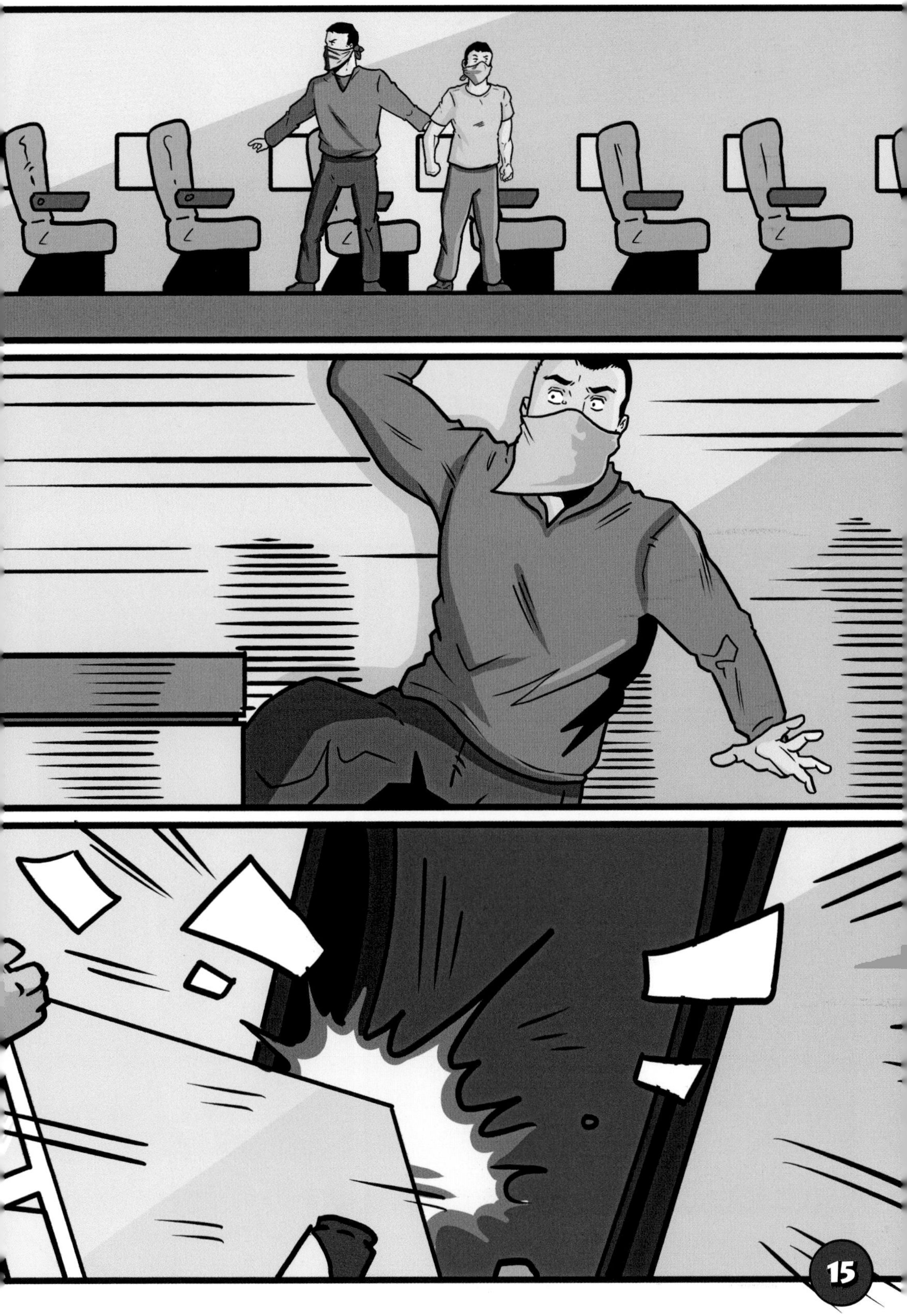

Chapter 3
HEROES IN ACTION

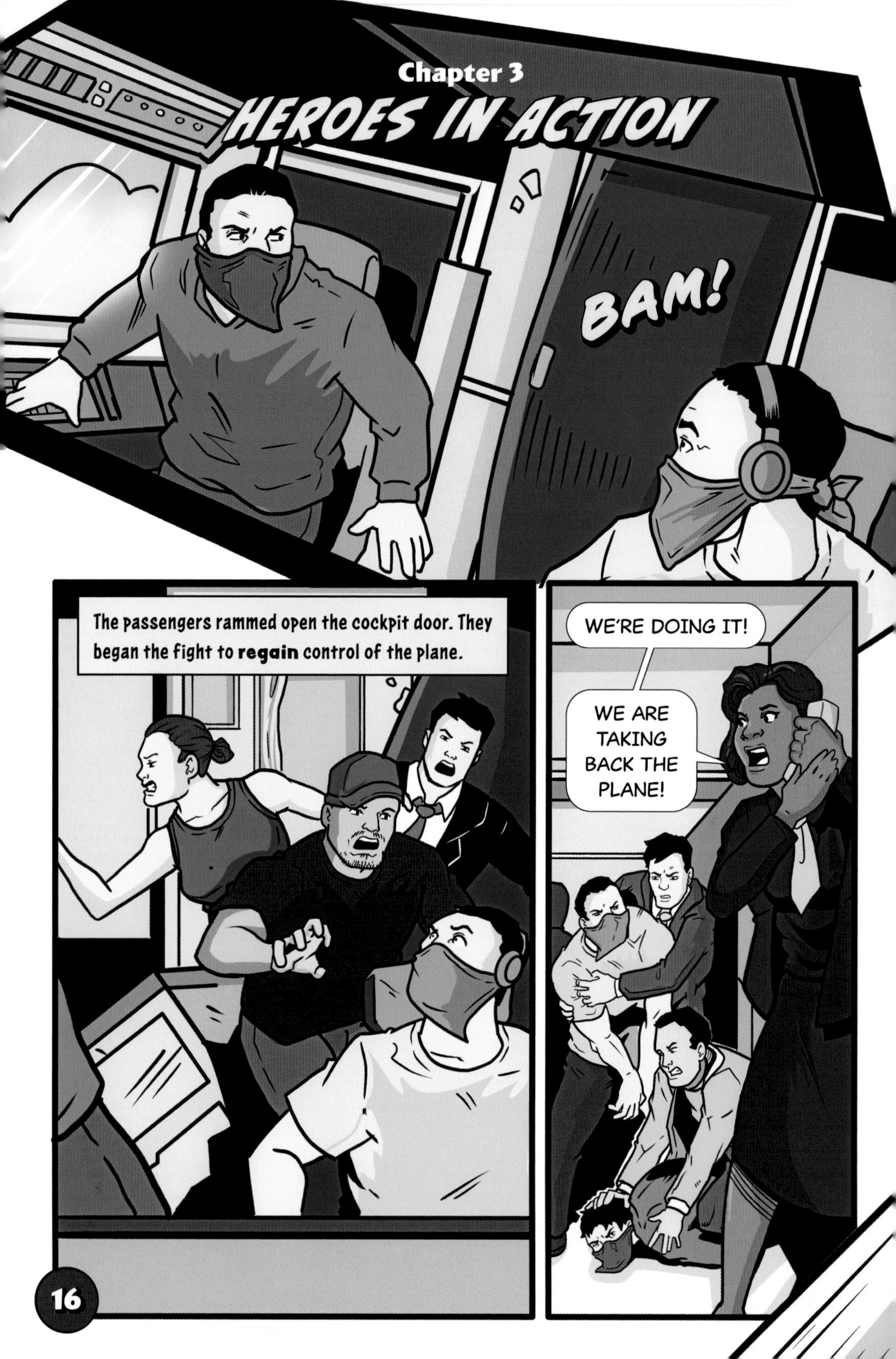
BAM!
The passengers rammed open the cockpit door. They began the fight to **regain** control of the plane.
WE'RE DOING IT!
WE ARE TAKING BACK THE PLANE!

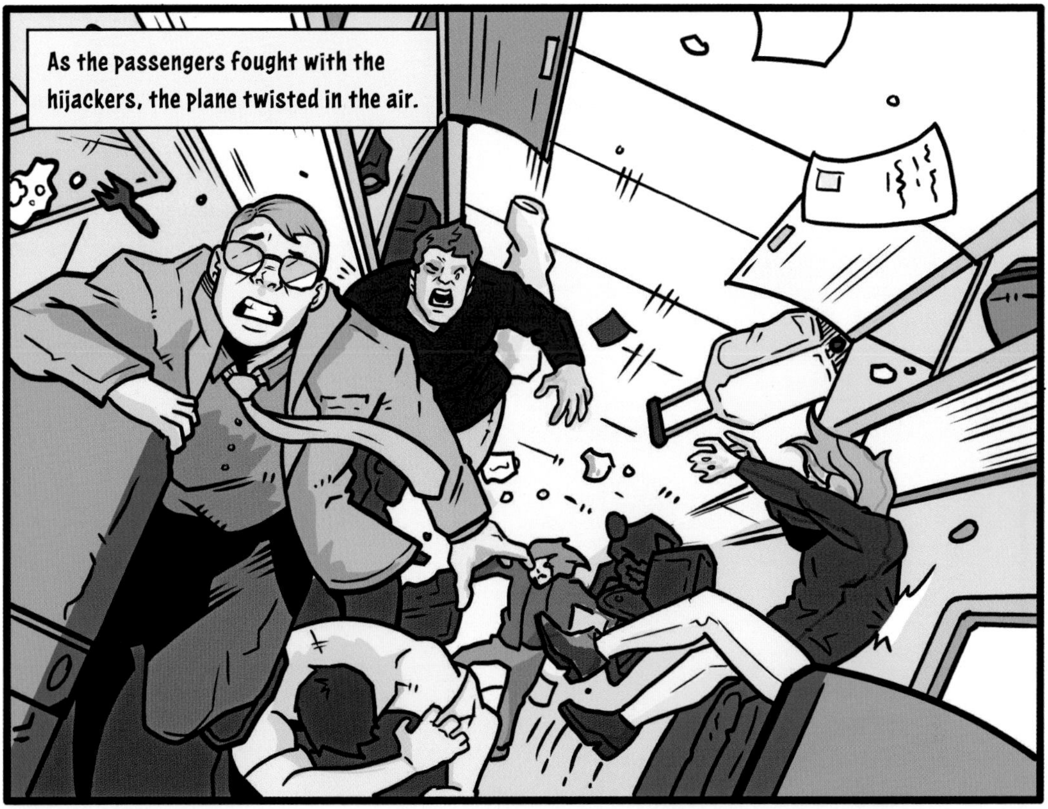
As the passengers fought with the hijackers, the plane twisted in the air.

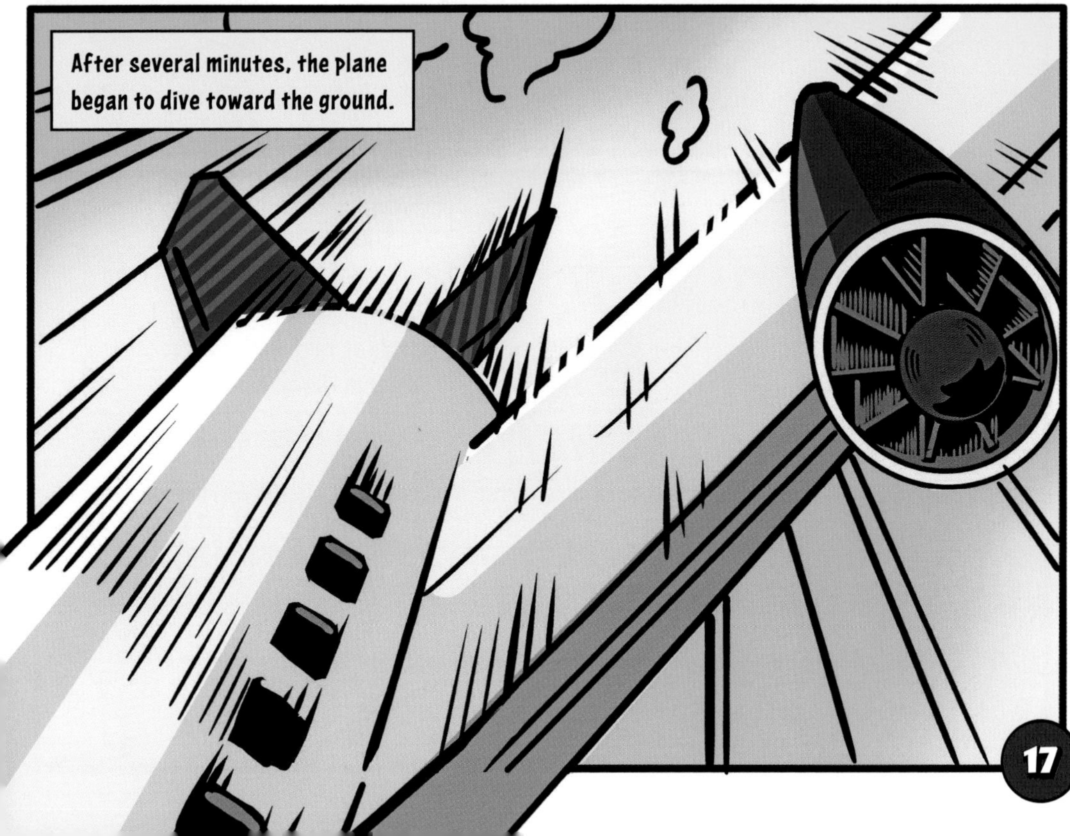
After several minutes, the plane began to dive toward the ground.

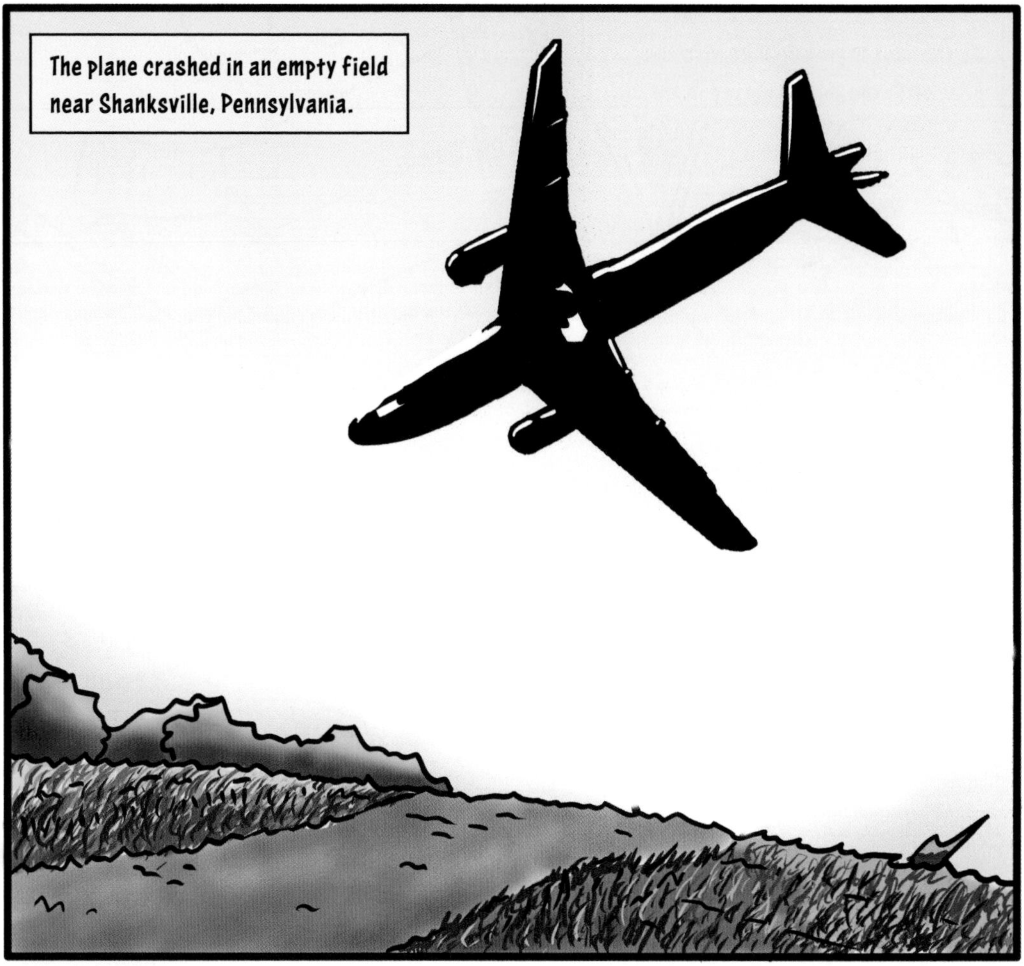
The plane crashed in an empty field near Shanksville, Pennsylvania.

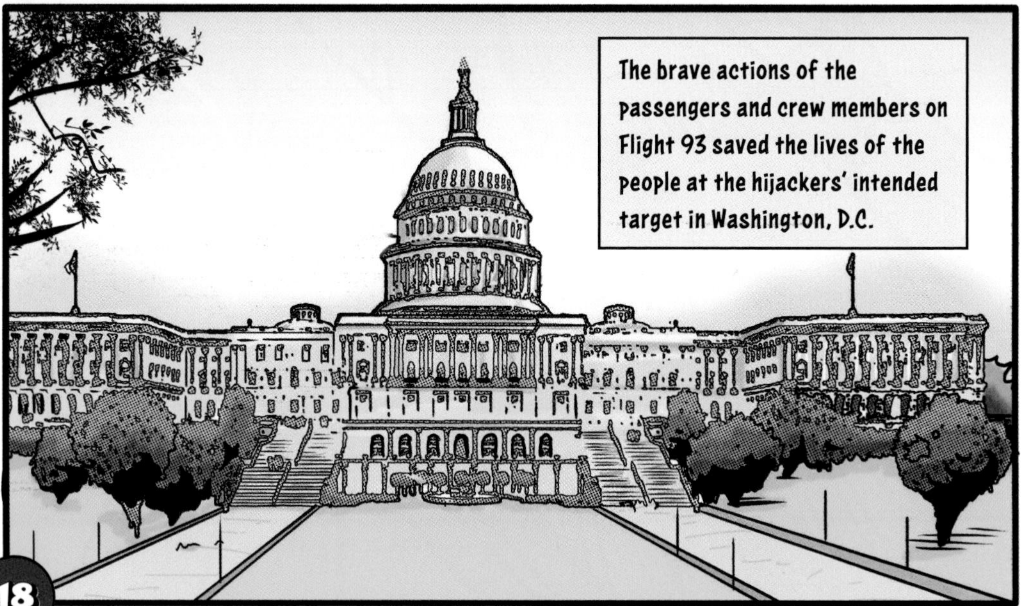
The brave actions of the passengers and crew members on Flight 93 saved the lives of the people at the hijackers' intended target in Washington, D.C.

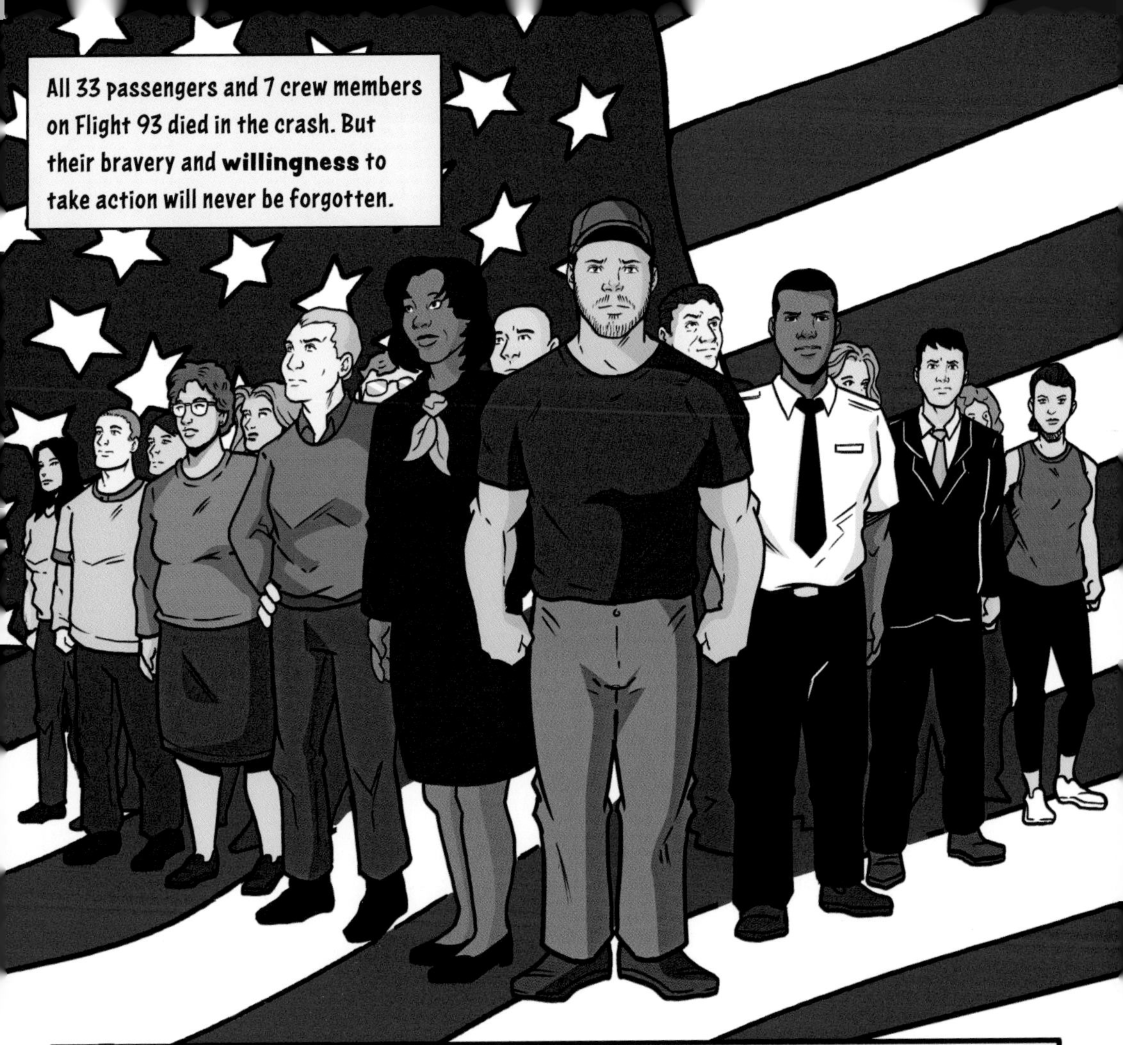
All 33 passengers and 7 crew members on Flight 93 died in the crash. But their bravery and willingness to take action will never be forgotten.

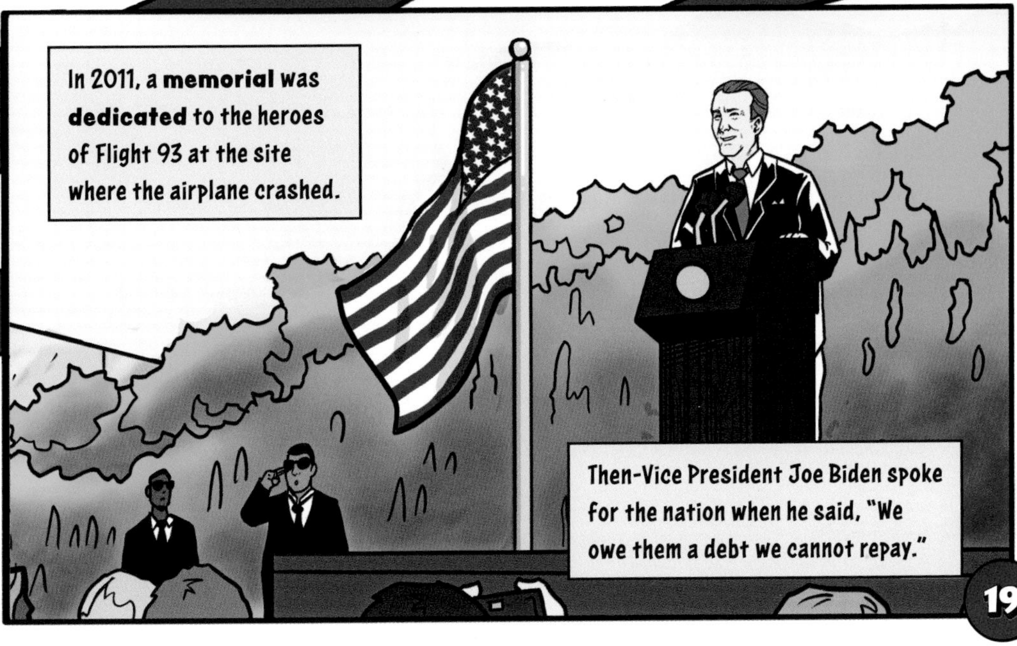
In 2011, a memorial was dedicated to the heroes of Flight 93 at the site where the airplane crashed.
Then-Vice President Joe Biden spoke for the nation when he said, "We owe them a debt we cannot repay."

A Day Like No Other

Tuesday, September 11, 2001, was a day that changed history. Groups of **terrorists** boarded four **domestic** flights in the United States. Not long after the planes took off, the attackers took over and began flying the planes.

At 8:46 a.m., terrorists steered the first plane into the north tower of the World Trade Center in New York City. Seventeen minutes later, the second plane was intentionally flown into the south tower of the World Trade Center. Both buildings were badly damaged and **engulfed** in flames. The crashes left the buildings so damaged that the towers would **collapse** before the morning was over.

At 9:37 a.m., the third plane was piloted into the side of the Pentagon building just outside Washington, D.C. The Pentagon, which is the headquarters of America's military forces, also caught fire.

Passengers on the fourth plane learned what had happened to the World Trade Center and the Pentagon. They decided to fight back and attempt to regain control of the plane. The plane for Flight 93 eventually crashed in an open field in Pennsylvania. Because of the actions of the passengers on this plane, the lives of countless people at the intended target in Washington, D.C., were saved.

In all, 2,977 people died from these attacks. Another 25,000 were injured. The devastation from these terrorist attacks is considered some of the worst in U.S. history.

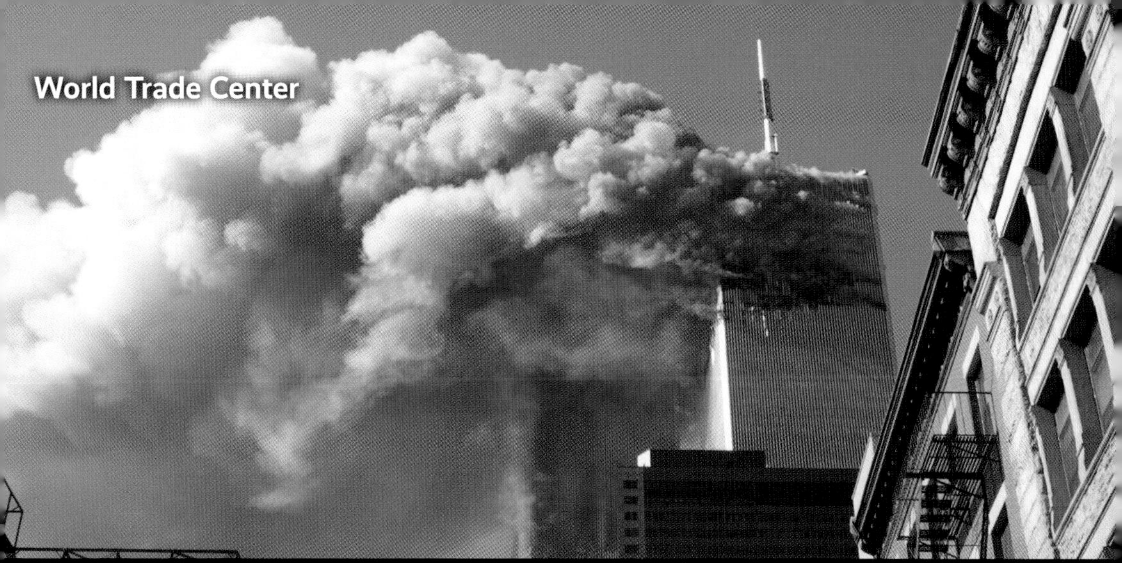
World Trade Center

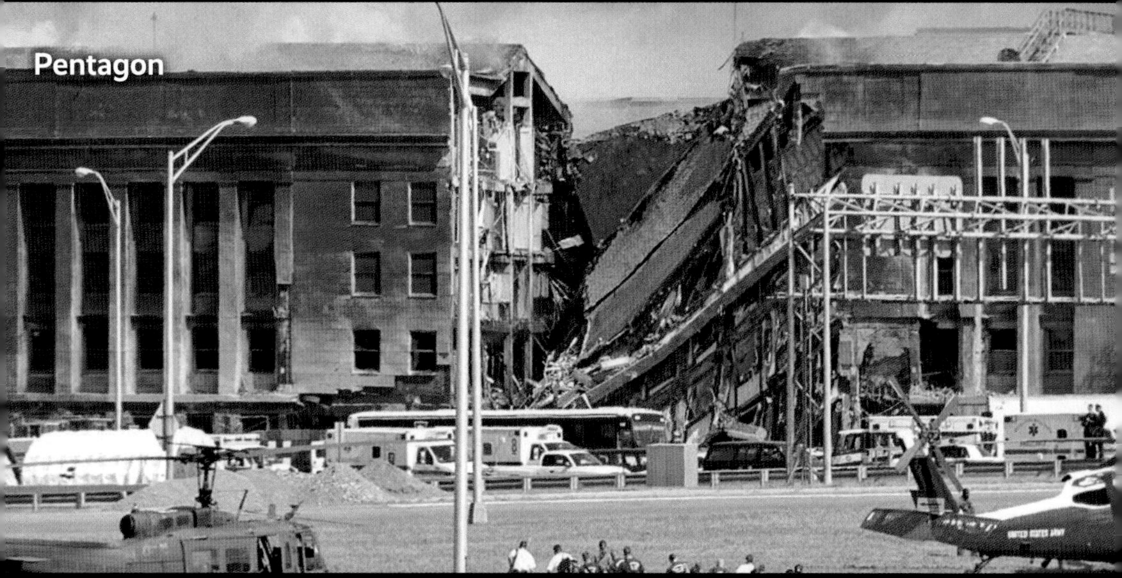
Pentagon

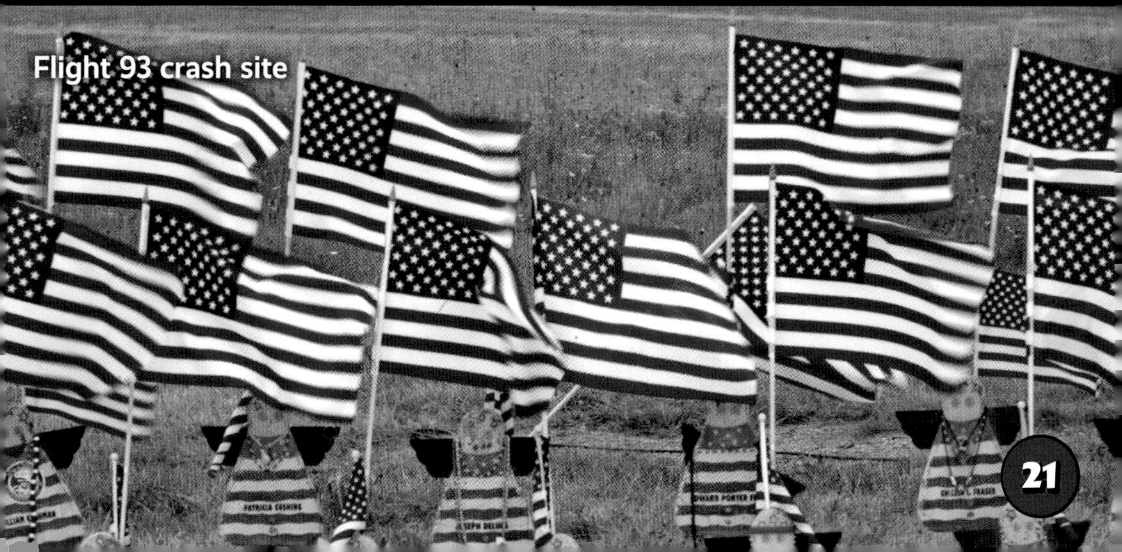
Flight 93 crash site

Other Flight 93 Heroes

While the passengers and crew members battled in the sky, others on the ground tried to help them prevent an even bigger tragedy.

Deena Burnett received a call from her husband, Tom, who was on the flight. She immediately called the FBI and filled them in on what Tom had said. When Tom called Deena back, she became a key source of information for the passengers and crew members. The information Deena gave them helped convince the Flight 93 passengers and crew members that they had to act to save the lives of others.

• • • • •

AirFone operator Lisa Jefferson also became a hero that day. She answered passenger Todd Beamer's call. Their conversation would later prove valuable to people trying to piece together what had happened. Lisa learned how many hijackers there were and what they had done. She listened to Todd as he told her about the people on board. Lisa's calm, brave work on the phone brought comfort and some answers to the passengers and crew members.

An AirFone

Glossary

AirFone a device in airplane seats that allowed passengers to make phone calls from the 1980s until the mid-2000s

alert watchful and ready

assistance aid or help

collapse to fall to the ground

dedicated officially made to honor or remember something or someone

destruction a lot of serious damage, usually to buildings

devastating very serious and awful

domestic inside a single country

engulfed completely covered by

hijacked taken over by force

mayday a radio call by a pilot indicating trouble or danger

memorial a place built to remember people who have died

overpower to defeat with a force much larger than the opponent's

regain to take back

terrorists people who use violence and threats to achieve their goals

willingness readiness to help or take part

Index

Read More

Forest, Christopher. *September 11th Attacks (Turning Points in U.S. History)*. Minneapolis: Jump! 2021.

Orr, Tamra B. *September 11 and Terrorism in America (A Modern Perspectives Book)*. Ann Arbor, MI: Cherry Lake, 2018.

Sanderson, Whitney. *The September 11 Attacks Transform America (Events that Changed America)*. Mankato, MN: Child's World, 2018.

Learn More Online

1. Go to **www.factsurfer.com**

2. Enter **"Fighting in Flight"** into the search box.

3. Click on the cover of this book to see a list of websites.